OFF THE BLOCK

VOLUME II

Quincy L. Lewis

DEDICATION

This book is about the city that raised me and countless others like myself. However, along with what the city and the experiences inspired by the city have taught me, I owe a lot to you. As I penned this second volume I imagined the confidence you'd always had in me even when I didn't have it in myself. Somehow you knew what I was capable of even when I didn't. Perhaps that's a gift of a big sister. I valued your opinions and you were always more than happy to provide them for me. Until we meet again, I will continue to make you proud and continue to write with the confidence that you have bestowed in me. This book is penned in your honor.

Angela Wallace 2012

CONTENTS

PART I

Poetry

PART II

SOCIAL COMMENTARY

ACKNOWLEDGMENTS

Special thanks to my mom and pops who have been
supporters of my dream since day one!

FOREWORD

Detroit, MI

Once called the Paris of the Midwest. The city that gave bi rth to the automobile and the Motown sound. It was also home to the famed Chambers Brothers and YBI. A city th at presents a unique experience of diversity and segregatio n at the same time. I love the city for the lessons it has tau ght me. I've seen young men grow up in the same neighbo rhood and one becomes successful at whatever they chase while another is conquered by the pursuit of street dreams. Quincy has presented what the city entails but he has done it in a variety of ways. Let him make you aware of the chall enges a man will face in this concrete jungle while simultan eously giving you the tools to survive as well as capitalize o n the lessons learned. Read it with an open mind. Finish it a changed human being.

By Derrick Q. Williams

POETRY

Musical Chairs

Anonymous to life I stay pinned to brown
wood
Women cry out and dance to the tune
Slow singing fills the room like oxygen
Yet, I can barely breathe.
The man in the box is definitely not
breathing
Life into the hollowness of empty souls
I retreat into the cocoon of my skin where
deep within
I feel the loneliness of a desperate soul
Seeking relevance in it all.
Barely catching sight from the abyss
But only this time.
Next time I would be closer, the singing
would be louder
Moving women to tears and dancing again
Men remain anonymous behind dark shades
Shielding portals to their souls
If indeed there are any souls to be shielded.
Next time comes sooner than last time
I'm even closer than before
Washed in waves of wailing and hollering
This time I feel it.

My chest rising then sinking then rising then
sinking
In rhythm with dancing women
Singing songs of sorrow while tears flush
sins from souls
She clutches my hand, her stern face shoot
daggers
I look through her as if she is not there,
unfazed by her stare
Then it smacks my face like several hands
There are no more rows ahead, no more
obstacles betwixt me and the box
Now I understand, but it's too late

I'm no longer looking from the behind the
dancing women
I'm looking from the front and others are
now looking at me
I plead, I beg, I now understand
But it's too late.

The Last First Sunday

Still tipsy from spirits the night before
Sunday had come too soon
Probably not soon enough

My eyes shut tight like an unforgiving
pickle jar
The phone, her voice, I turn away, eyes still
clinched
Forcing the words from my dried lips
A few hours ago sipped the very nectar
That should swing me first through church
doors
"I'm not going," words squeaking through
the cracks
Not knowing the fate of today, I fall again to
slumber
Only to be awaken by an unexplainable
force
Tinkering synaptic cords in my brain
pressing me
Forward from sin induced rest, back to
yesterday's
Clothes for today.
No thought about tomorrow
I head to church in haste, knowing I'm late
From behind marvelous hats, over babies'
screams
I found her.
She and my mother sat close, wind of the
sermon
Blew through their hair as notes swam the
waves

Of prosperity, hope and divinity.
I'm glad I made it here, happy to see my
sister
Happy to see my mother, happy to see our
Father

As Sunday rinsed the sins of Saturday away
I rushed to them after service, she smiled in
peace
I returned the favor, service was the void
that filled
An empty space and my soul was thankful
We talked for a moment then parted ways
Plans of watching our favorite Lions had
been made
The sun got lower as did my eyes, choosing
home
Over travel I lay deep in couch cushions a
lazy breeze
Slowly lulling me to sleep. I never made it.
The next day awaken by shrieks from
downstairs
My half sleep brain determining the words.
Between pants, shirt, shoes, somehow
finding myself
Whizzing the street behind the wheel
worried

That she was gone and indeed she was gone.
On to the next stage, soul slipped away
while sleeping
I sulked silently still wishing I had come to
watch Lions
Linger in losses because I have lost and now
I'm lost
But I spent first Sunday with my sister last
Sunday
Now our Sundays are no more.

Boyz N The Hood

Them boys around my way up all night
Might creep through and silence pimp juice
on sight
Pain in their hearts
Menace in their souls
Shine bright like a diamond but no Rhianna
song
Singing silence simply suspect
No expectations to prosper
No expectations to transcend
No expectations at all.
But how do we dig deep dividing

Not conquering the conquest

A boy indigenous to his surroundings who
has been told for so long
That he is not the King in which he is
Unbeknownst to them
Hidden in plain sight from us
Despite the illusion that they are meek
We are burdened with responsibility
Feeding them with knowledge of their worth
Until them boys become these men.

Solitary Confinement

We talked about everything from sports to
women
Countless hours of NFL Films
documentaries
I never knew who Gayle Sayers was before
then
Hours behind the free throw line draining
Buckets upon buckets like rain drops from
the sky
On my way back to school I said I would be
back
Not knowing that you wouldn't be there

Did you know you weren't going to be
there?
I'm pissed just a little because we had more
laughs
We had more discussions, we had more time
So I thought
Never thinking before I returned you would
have returned
To that light that I've heard illuminates
Minds and souls inviting them to what lies
beyond
I guess I just want to know why

Is that selfish? Am I wrong for curiosity?
What compels a man to finalize his own
future?
So many questions, not enough answers
Confusion fills up like inner tubes in BMX
bikes
We used to ride up and down the block
Terrorized by Caesar in the front lawn
unchained
We pedaled faster, he would laugh louder
Now that laugh is gone and so is he
I said I would be back

Why didn't you tell me you wouldn't be
there to see?

145th And Lennox

Opportunity arrives so I rush through the
door
No navigation, no compass, no map
Just ambition
Eyes bright like sunshine early morning
On fresh snow in the winter time
Cast off to a concrete jungle
People jammed in small confines
Never apologizing for intruding personal
spaces
Up all night and all day
Shirt and tie on the #2 train downtown
From uptown where Frank and Nicky
Made millions off desperate souls
Searching for silence
Heads filled with frantic screams
treacherous torment
Chains on ankles broken decades ago
Replaced by shackles on the mind

I break free, shackles burst into pieces
behind me
One step ahead of the other fast into futures
Yet to be passed but eventually become the
past
And new futures must be spawned
Before all is forgotten
Strides grow longer down 5th Ave
Lennox Lounge in the distance
Black Enterprise in close range
I have arrived and so it begins
As quickly as it started, it had come to an
end
My experiences stay etched in my mind like
graffiti
On bodegas closed for the evening
Flight returns me to my block miles away
from Liberty
Where she stands upright with a torch
Less than a month later the towers came
down
Only a short distance from where my
dreams blew up.

Protect And Serve

911 is a joke
Chuck D and Flav spit that in our ear
Many years ago and today is still true
Cube said FUCK THE POLICE decades ago
From beneath the foot of law we feel the
same pain
Law enforcement enforces its will
Upon my melanin brothers and sisters
Voices silenced by batons
Lives erased by department issued

Pistols beat down by shields
Once used to protect, now imposing power
Hungry blue pigs igniting riots in Baltimore
Ferguson and Detroit two times back in the
days
Leaving communities in a daze
Never resurfacing the abyss of disdain
Cloaked by waves of blue uniforms
Washed by years of brutality
Even with our hands up
Fighting for last breaths
Running for our lives

Knowing our rights
We hang in cells
We hang in cells.

Three Fifths

Once were mighty Kings and Queens
Land and fortune at fingertips
Pointing to the equinox
Calculated beyond mortal comprehension
Still to this day unknown and unproven
Centuries before civilization
Casually castrated our manhood
Shipping us like cattle to a land of
opportunity
Filled with white puffs purely for profits
While sun beats down like swift night sticks
In broad daylight
We are invisible

Sitting on backs of busses
Hanging from trees
Before marching on through Montgomery
Sealing the caskets of Martin and Malcolm

Hoping that the dream stays alive by any
means
Necessary to survive because once we were
three fifths
Now three fifths into bottles of hope trying
to subdue
Realities set by history and a burden of truth
That lies to us all.

KIDS

Laughter sprawled across skies
Limitless with nuances of Spring
Starting again never seeing the end result
Pressures from every angle appear invisible
Inside globes of false snow in the South Pole
St. Nick sips milk and crunches cookies
Sliding down chimneys, but wait,
Ain't no chimneys on Six Mile and Hoover
But six miles from the Hoover
Damn, it's the same thing
I guess I'm just bitter and old
Memories of playing tag in the streets

Fading finally into the rear-view mirror
Giving way to the road ahead
Move not in haste, enjoy the scenery

Once it's gone, it's gone forever.

Erasable Ink

The book has been written
Millions of words straddle edges of paper
Bound by experiences, memories and
lessons learned
Behaviors between brothers
Bothersome to say the least
Unity broken in chapters
Introductions flip frantically to conclusions
Considering good reads often go quickly
Minds barely soak up sense
Before abruptly coming to an end
There is no sequel
There is no Volume II
No more pages to turn
Even when stories seem incomplete

Under The Weather

Sun rays beating down on backs
Beads of sweat roll like tumble weeds down
Desolate deserted diaries
Destined in disgust and disregard
But still we swing low
Sweet chariot
And we still ain't been carried home
Forty acres short, care less about the mule
Broken skin, broken hearts, broken promises
Surrounded by soft white clouds
Seducing us into slumber
Sipping suddenly the serenity of false hope
Promise of prosperity
Bound by a letter
Written by some Willie Lynch man
Will he Lynch men?
That is the question
Answers untold, somehow lost in ancient
folklore
Inscriptions in pyramids larger than life
Hidden in plain sight so we walk blindly
Into darkness with a glimmer of light

At the end of tunnels that never end
Prosperity that never comes
Acres that never add up to forty
A promised land that never materializes
A dream that never comes true
Langston, I ask, what happens to that dream
anyway?

Fear

Eating from within hollowed wells
Deep beneath shields that shelter us
From outside forces destroying
Our motivation
Questioning our desire
Forcing our hand
Often folding when we indeed have the best
hand
No matter the cards, it fatigues our faith
Depletes our capacity of confidence
Finally shutting the door of opportunity
Once knocking furiously
Vanishes suddenly into an abyss of
nonexistence
We grow weary

Fight fleeting in the wind
Like kites twisted by nature's whisper
Tossed through intersections of clouds
Before crashing violently to the ground.

In The Clouds

Nerves tense like murderers on trial
Jury sitting patiently waiting to punish
Searching for a release
Release from pain
Release from suffering
Release from reality
Rolled tightly pinched from both ends
I inhale
Waiting to exhale
Aroma serenades the ailing nerves
Bringing them to rest
Once disturbed by life's plentiful discretions
I inhale
Waiting to exhale
Until numbness fills my nerves
Only to return another day.

King's Court

Kings and queens and gold things
Marvelous structures unexplained by human
knowledge
Alignment with celestial formations
Peak even the most inquisitive minds
Kingdoms and fortune an eternity before
much created
Yet, no thought given has provoked our own
thirst
For truths that lie betwixt false enamored
fiction
Aged crumbling pages serve as carriers
Though the water flows deep
Unrivaled by currents
Somehow we've grown complacent
Willing to ignore the passage forged by
generations
Upon generations fatigued with mountains
Stones and boulders on shoulders
Manufactured to manufacture our very
existence
Today, yesterday and days to come
So what have we overcome?
Questions multiply to no certain degree

Much like numbers created in pyramids
magically
Mimicking equations and principles not yet
discovered
Or so it seems.
That knowledge is sacred, powerful and
hidden
In plain sight we see not what's intended
For our own misfortune has formed blinders
upon eyes
Open wide but never seeing
Truly seeing what treasure we've ascended
Only seeing the misfortune we have created
Soon we shall once again prosper in
positivity
No longer sulking in solitude
Rising to the thrown as kings and queens
once again.

75 South

75 South homeward bound
Where she's from
Dirt roads and evil skeletons
Holding sacred to visions of past
misfortunes

Buried under southern hospitality
Hidden in broken vernacular
Humble beginnings carve strength in her
face
Reflections of chickens and hogs scurrying
Fretfully about her grandfather's yard
No colored allowed
Whites only
Pressures of black obscurity mold her short
stature
Resilience makes her twelve feet tall
Windows to her soul bear witness
To many moons of modest mundane
melancholy
Brought forward from generations past
Plantations plotted, polarizing
Possibilities disappearing into thin air
Yet her skin stays simply amazing
Never giving any hint of her time spent on
Earth's
Green pastures corroded by humanity's
disposition
And yet, she musters enough energy to smile
Bringing life to her youngest child
For that I am honored
Pleased beyond probable conception

My heart owes gratitude, for she who made
me
Made me who I am today.

Oglethorpe

Miles past Atlanta off in dusty dirt roads
A house sits sturdy on land owned by
generations
Past and future, thus holding way for
representation
For generations to come
Tucked away from highways traversing
urbanized decay
Leading into a grove planted with seeds of
yesteryear
Grown into flowers of today
Once loomed so colossal in my mind
Reduced to a miniature version of what I
envisioned
Many years before
Black presidents and wealthy black business
owners

Made Montezuma men think anything was
possible
Unbeknownst to most and draped by a
mental cloak
Disguised ever so slightly to escape
detection
And hold the slave in shackles with no
actual chain
Reactions go unnoticed
Drenched in false serenity
Somehow satisfied with how life has stalled
Dropped anchors hold fast to what has been
No less imprisonment than Alcatraz
Minus physical bars
Personified by classist greed of a country
Born off sweat from brows
Former kings and queens
Attempting to erase mental recollection
After being reduced to a month of 29 days
As if not short changed enough
Scholastic pages disintegrated
Flames extinguished once burned so bright
As the north star that pointed to freedom
Existence lay precious on shoulders strapped
Slinging cotton worn on streets laced in
blood

Leaked from bodies fallen prey to savages,
No regard
To life, just a name on cotton once picked
by scorned
Persecuted hands placed together praying
for a future
We hardly respect with no respect to what
has granted
What we often take for granted.

Prison Bars

Locked in by levels unknown
Caged like birds, but ain't no singin'
I wonder how she thought she knew
Queen Angelou much respect due
Through verses and rhymes
Trying to free our minds
Held captive in chains
Mental and physical remains
Hollerin' and screamin' go tell it on the
mountain
Sisters and brothers forced to use another
fountain

Jimmy's Blues and Langston Hughes
Gwendolyn Brooks gave us hints and clues
Keys from pages of words to set us free
Understanding the true meaning of what it is
to be
Of giants, kings and queens
Having Good Times in Cabrini Greens
Struggles real as pyramids loom
Jewels bling from King Tut's tomb
Distant memories of treasures beyond belief
Sent angels like Martin while his existence
was brief
All in an effort to remind us freedom of
mind
Allows freedom of soul
And freedom of soul allows us to shine.

Two-Hand Touch

Four of us playing football in the street
Passes to the outside
Runs to the inside
All laughs, fun and all
Moving to the side to let cars breeze by

Continuing our quest for the Super Bowl
Championship
From the NFL
Neighborhood Football League
Barely in double digits of life
We parade the streets like professional
athletes
Hurrying to the side, a black van whizzes by
We hop back to the middle of the street
Continuing our game, black van still there
A few houses down,
Men burst from the doors like lava
Spewing into the street
Our game paused we hit the start button
Guns drawn ambushing the door
Demanding entry
Her aged frame shook nervously in the door
Staring down barrels
Of life snatching cannons
We stand still
Time stands still
Tear through the house looking for evidence
Tying her son to drugs trafficked
To line the pockets
Not of his, but America's who hid behind

"Say No To Drugs" while supplying our
neighborhood
Same drugs forcing us to fight amongst one
another
Sounds like Africa with diamonds, but no
diamonds here
Just hardened coal unearthed but never
understanding
What lies beneath is that same diamond
Cut precisely, slightly imperfect perfection
Finding nothing, yet leaving her home in
shambles
Retreating to their chariot with no regard
Tears flow like a river running it's natural
course
Raging and forging along terrain tested by
time
Anger emerges
Her son has brought danger to her door step
Swallowed by the streets spit out by society
Lost in a calm destruction.

White Devil

Remembering seeing her from the street
passing by
I looked twice and knew I had to have her
We whipped through the turnaround to get
back to her
Leaping from the passenger side
Giving the wheels no time to bring us to a
halt
I dashed to her side
People laughed, but I saw her beauty
Smoke and all I was willing to ignore
Because she eclipsed my heart
Shielding it from desire of any other.
I was enthralled with passion
Only to be captured in her full body
She would be my first
Lasting impressions on my soul
Doing everything I could to savor her tender
touch
Plush in every way
Soft and supple with a tough exterior
My oh my I still think of you some times
My white devil
Devious and adventurous
Peaking my inner-beast allowing me to
release

Through all of the curves and bumps
She rides and I rise
Above the limit before pulling back and
slowing down
Because maybe we're moving too fast
As soon as I let you out of my sight
You were taken away from me
Never seeing you again until one day I get a
call
I rush to the yard and I recognized you from
the back
But everything else was a mess
I felt empty, empty inside
For my love had been taken away and
abused
Nothing left to give, nothing left to receive
I glanced one more time before turning
away
Leaving behind her memory
A distant faded reflection of my past.

48205

Where I'm from, the FEDS got eyes peeled
Like bananas for monkeys slipping

Sliding through the streets that watch
silently
Duped by democracy designed to destroy
Our very being while we allow it to do so
Much for so little effort given to push our
own
Democracy inside our hood that is invisible
Yet in plain sight, at least when the news is
bad
Suddenly appear out of thin air, curlers,
missing teeth
Fumbling over words skipped by subpar
education
Classrooms packed with forty-five brains in
thirty desks
One teacher with half a paycheck going out
of her way
Out of her mind trying to reach two or three
that may
Or may not break the cycle of an epidemic
plaguing
A city with promise but no one promised
Another day getting gas one night and losing
your life
In exchange for pennies that won't buy your
freedom

Won't buy your justice
Won't buy your relevance in a place that
steps over you
Like puddles in streets laced with gold
And you have no fortune
Just the misfortune of a less fortunate place
in life
Where houses disappear like thieves in the
night
Dope retails like merchandise in department
stores
For soul searching vessels in need of an
escape
In search of destinations for destiny
Because they were destined to destroy
barriers
But tripped up by life's shoestrings
Tumble to pavements painted in blood.

Politics and Pimpin'

Pimped out to plantations
Power plays, poetic prophecies
Once a ploy to trick our minds
Making chains seem like opportunity

Shackles like solutions
Questioning answers of it all
Cocaine moving through veins
Major arteries of major cities
Leaving trails of menace through our
societies
Boys in the hood lookin' for the juice.

Marching To The Beat

Feet tread lightly on concrete
Sloshing through smut
Splashing violently to curbs
Where innocence is squandered in disregard
Melanin holding us hostage behind bars of
racism
We shall overcome, at least that's what
Martin said
And we're still searching for the Promised
Land.

Trapped in the Trap

No way out
Several ways in
Doubt and fear leave souls destined to be
destroyed
In search of notes left by presidents
Serving no precedence or prevalence
In the grand scheme of things
Grand schemes and things
Ruin neighborhoods
Consume families
Make prison pockets obese
Cemeteries run out of plots placing price
tags
On toe tags, tip-toeing through the tulips no
longer
Lights dimmed in the dining room
Sorry we're closed
Sign flipped like birds to the world that
created them
Pushing the promise of prosperity
Never truly prospering
Maybe this is what it is
What it was
What it will always be

No voice shedding light where darkness has
invaded
Staging a coup in the corrupted government
inside
Brains washed by media, circumstance
Relentless beckoning from the streets
Starving to devour the aimless
Feeding on the greed of unknowing vessels
Equipped with batteries lodged in backs
As they are no longer in control
Just being controlled.

Interstate 80

Caution to the wind
Opportunity shining in the distance
Humming of concrete birds lull
apprehension to sleep
Until finally it is gone
Perhaps too late to look back
Too soon to rush forward
Just the right time to
Just the right time to
Sputter along in search of the next
destination

Fear of the unknown marks territory
Within minds running through mines
Fretful of detonation sending everything into
space
Maneuvering mile after mile
Finish line finally coming into view
A million miles from normal
Whatever that is anyway
Because I don't know normal
Never had the pleasure of meeting her
I hear she's beautiful, though most have
never seen her
A fabled tale of folklore
Renditions of rhetoric passed through
generations
We all aspire to come in contact
Sometimes Waiting For Godot like Beckett

Loud Silence

Filling rooms of synaptic closets
Forcing way into hollowed space
Consuming every inch of capacity
Until pots boil over
Spilling to the bowels of our souls

Trapped by hooks clawing continuously
So fierce the pain excruciating and relentless
Only cries for mercy seep out in tiny weeps
But who will give us mercy?
For thine eyes have seen not what they were
intended
Our ears have heard not what was prescribed
Heart strings snap with tension stretched
until
Tiny threads hang on for dear life
Dear life
I'm in love with you and though I don't treat
you as such
Despite temptation to stray, I beg for you to
stay
Clocks slicing away at us consistently
Murdering one second at a time and they
never return
I will never get them back no matter how
hard I attempt
Holding on until knuckles turn white
Lights nearing the end of the tunnel
Frantically pumping brakes no longer
functioning
Alas, too weary to wreak havoc any longer

I leave you behind now, my love, until we meet again.

Just Plane Crazy

Serenity of morning shining brightly
Amidst stages she holds her torch high
Burning desires of freedom, emancipation
A proclamation of the such
Indeed a gift honoring her independence
In the backdrop, twins hold steady
Wings from sinister beginnings
A convergence of the twain
Sparking Hardy's thirst for Titanic
Sized wreckage on land leaving shadows
Where the twins once stood tall
Under the light of her torch
Begging for answers
Questions unknown, lost in smoke
Filled lungs laying foundations
Cancerous perhaps
Rotting the inner workings
Blind folded by media controlled responses
Covered in blood of non-existing existence
Smoke and mirrors.

Chain Gang

Linked by ankles
Tied by wrists
Unable to maneuver without one or the other
One tug from the leg and we all fall down
Single file, bound together
By chains and shackles
Relentlessly forcing together
What was once separate
Conjoined by despair
Intertwined by fear
A culture not quite grasping the idea
Of equity, equality and equal rights
If one sees a way out we must all go
Once the chain yanks we're left no choice
How magnificent the harmony if we moved
In unison with one another
The chains would have no effect
So while we may not be able to break chains
Perhaps we learn to move with them
With one another.

Devil's Night

Bursting into celebrations of homecoming
Soldiers from a war not their own
Coming back home to the same disrespectful
Condescending flag he was defending
Abroad, yet Detroit is burning from within
Racial tensions boiled over a steaming pot
Spurring fires on 12th
Destruction to hearts and businesses
Never returning decades later
But we cringe when Kwame makes deals
With family and friends
Money circulates against their will
Now suddenly an ear ring and hip-hop rep
Is a disgrace to a city rotten with corruption
Red-lined encryptions invisible to most
But clear as crystals shimmering in winter
To those who traverse the remnants of 12th
South of 8 Mile where people think Detroit
But if you ain't from Detroit
I see how Hollywood makes you think
Much like the media makes us all think
Incapable of individual thought
Progressive thinking is what begs silence
Like our fallen leaders who

Silenced by the machine
Working in tandem with our own neglect
Wielding a beast so savage inside
Once let loose
It can be amazing or destructive.

Strip Tease

Packed pews
Overstuffed parking lots
Choirs singing for His mercy
Salvation slingers selling saves
Enslaved to the hypocrisy of some
Who think they break down doors Sunday
Suddenly spares their souls
But what is the visit without intent
Malice in hearts can't be cloaked
By congregation's charming charades

On Vacation

He don't see the block much no more
Three hots and a cot
Brainwashed by society's mirror
Nails dirty from digging
The scene with a gangsta lean
Mug shots like graduation photos
All caps no gowns
On papers with no paper
Sometimes he likes to take a trip
Get away from metal and concrete
See what's going on in the hood.
Ain't seen him in a while
Maybe enjoying his own piece of mind
Not peace of mind
Knowing he'd rather have a piece of mine
A slice of my life
A portion of my pie
And I have the nerve to frown
When things get tough and doors shut
Like cell bars clang
Inmates hit resets buttons to do it all again
Groundhog's Day
Indeed we are creatures of habits
Sometimes bad

When he's on vacation its good for a while
Then it's calling him like crack did Pookie
Soul tarnished, hate to see him go
I know he's just on vacation

Other Side of The Game

Cartier frames
Rubber bands and bills
Ice dancing in lights like strippers on poles
Paying for school, everybody's Diamond
Until St. Louis blew up the spot
Making it rain presidents who fucked
Our very existence
But still flood floors with their remanence
Gold bottles like royalty

Look closer, wipe the lens and focus

White bricks and elbows of earth's green
Sedate societies into a senseless abyss
Families left traumatized
Seeds planted only a few years prior
Never have chances to sprout

Cut down by selfish greed
Birthed by struggle turned hustle
While inside wombs tormented
By the same means making her drop
Drop it like it's hot as steel when it blast
Predestined to lose, prepared to fail
Duck taped in tears
Reversing and forwarding in thought
Coming up with no answers to equations
Making no equation to what's to come
Turned up with turncoats
Then too late to react
Strapped up and slapped up

Wipe the lens again

See it clear as diamonds
On Cartier frames
Rubber bands and bills.

Quiet Thought

Pressures of it all weigh heavy
Heart searching for reasons to beat
Maybe it's easier to check out

From a world unknowing of my existence
Uncaring of tiny fractures threatening to
break my very foundation
Crumbling at the source
How wonderful would it be to be invisible
Subtract myself from life's equation
Mysteries of what lies beyond white lights
Shining deeply, piercing my soul's
Release to the final resting place
Or if it's even a place for resting at all
Trying to escape the grasp of utter chaos
But drowning in an abyss of torment
One pull of the trigger, triggering thoughts
Remorse...Bang!
It's too late.

Where's The Love

Ain't no love here, not no more
Rage brought hasty hands from Hastings
Paradise Valley and Black Bottom
Extinguished by gentrification
Souls of seasons passed
Lost in winds of truth and deceit

Black Lives Matter

Beaten to death
Hanged in prisons
Robbed of our very last breath
Plantations predicted from our past
Punishment seems to be prevalent futures
Untold, yet warned from the bowels of Jesus
Jamestown where slaves come ashore
Owned by he who translated stone tablets of
Hebrews unbeknownst to even themselves
Centuries later we still are confused, waiting
While a man sits 19 feet tall enshrined as if
His emancipation meant much more than
Pennies stamped with his likeness
In masses that won't respect my likeness
With my hands up
When I can't breathe
If I have a hoodie on
Don't peer down your nose
When I say our lives matter
Unless you don't agree
Embedded in melanin deficient minds
Portraits of Kunta etched into memory

Wild animals, blood dripping from teeth
Cut on flesh of despair and meat of freedom
We might never see
Like promised land Martin dreamed dearly
Despite his demise...
We just want our lives to matter
And we must also confront the mirror
Whose reflection reminds of self-hatred
Spawn by centuries of absent freedom
Chaining ourselves with shackles
Shaped by our own mental captivity
We must also know that our lives matter.

American Dream

Two kids, a dog, white picket fences
Political freedom, pursuit of happiness
Cotton fields and plantations
Promises of freedom never redeemed
Like coupons with expired dates
Bills hold faces of forefathers
While four fathers bury four daughters
Erased by hate wrapped in white sheets
Pure as America the Beautiful

But how beautiful is she?
An American Dream
What happens to a dream deferred?
Martin told us he had a dream
A dream we all endured with hopes
Equality would rain like tears from the Son
Alas, Langston indeed I ask,
What does happen to a dream deferred?
Does it explode?

The Block

Concrete jungles
We animals in here
Blood dripping from teeth
Carcasses cast to curbs
Savage souls surrender
To nothing
From nothing
We rise from ashes
Of blunts burned beneath
Broken dreams
Broken families
Broken trust
Broken windows

Broken promises
Dashed dreams daring
A dying breed
To break the chains
Disguised in platinum and gold
Signs of fame and fortune
For less fortunate
Foes failed in falls
Sprung from summers
Where we once played ball in streets
Midnight games of hide and seek
The homie couldn't play on Saturdays
One day sooner than our Sabbath Days
Running to the yard playing hoops
Until dusk missing dates for dances
Due to him having next
Times we spent whole days in basements
Playing video games until getting dizzy
Darting outside to inhale fresh air
Dope boys beat down the street
Disappearing into the night
Leaving behind remnants of bass on crack
Rocks we threw from beneath dumpsters
In alleys soaked with piss and rat droppings
Before running inside after street lights
Shed light to our block

Revealing what lies in darkness
We run to try to beat the speed of the light
Some of us never made it home
Falling prey to the streets that raised us.

Quincy L. Lewis

OFF THE BLOCK : VOLUME II

Quincy L. Lewis

SOCIAL CRITICISM

Do Black Lives Matter?

A routine stop can lead to your last breath. I have to be honest in saying that the flashing blue and red lights bring beads of sweat to my palms and forehead. Sometimes when they pull behind me with the lights flashing, I pull to the side and if they whiz by me in pursuit of another vehicle, I find myself visibly trembling. Even if the radio is at a high volume, I can hear my heart beating over the sound of music. The lunacy of it all is overbearing because my license is valid, my driving record is clean, I've got insurance coverage and I have no priors. So, why do I panic?

Power of Authority

Too many instances, I've seen black men and black women parish at the hands of overzealous law enforcement. Eric Garner pled for his life after declaring that he was no longer able to breathe while being pounced on by several officers. Spencer Lee McCain was gunned down by Baltimore County police who claimed he was wielding a gun and of course no gun was ever found. Freddy Gray died after receiving internal injuries from unnecessary force used by 6 officers while arresting him. Michael Brown who, even though it was not proven that he had his hands in a surrendering position, could have been detained without firing as many shots into him as the officer did. Not to mention the South Carolina officer who was caught on camera shooting Walter Scott while he was running away from him, then tossing a weapon near his fallen body to implicate some sort of threat and corroborate his story. Luckily someone was recording this, but why does there have to be a video?

The Eye In The Sky

In football, coaches always say, the eye in the sky doesn't lie. Just meaning that they have it on film and once you see the film there can be no denying it. Unfortunately, that is not the case for black people and police. Even while being recorded we can be violated, belittled and killed with no repercussions. It's utterly despicable to swallow the harsh truth that law enforcement has taken its role of enforcement to a level that is unacceptable. It's no secret that I have seen white individuals do YouTube videos holding assault rifles and refusing to present identification only to walk away at the end of the video with no arrest or citation. Yet, that same law enforcement regime will make a routine traffic stop where an unarmed black person could lose his life.

The Trust is Gone

The gang of the boys in blue. The pigs. Whatever you refer to them, they have got to respect a black life. It is deplorable, to say the least, that I should be reduced to a sweaty mess when police are in my presence. Not because I'm a convicted felon on the run. Not because I have an illegal amount of drugs on me or in the vehicle that I'm driving. Not because I've done anything other than demand my respect as a human being and request the same information as to why I've been stopped that any of my white counterparts can demand

and receive without ever being detained, humiliated or killed. Only because I'm black and somehow the threat of my blackness has made you either react in fear or impose your authority on me until I tuck in my humanity and allow you to bask in your fictitious superiority.

Where's The Social In Social Media?

Social media has taken the world by storm. Back in the day it was College Club. Black Planet. Myspace. Now, of course you've got Facebook, Twitter, Instagram and SnapChat just to name a few. Anyone and everyone can be whoever they want to be behind cell phones and laptops. The funny thing is that the "Social" part of social media is actually the part that's missing. With interactions like these made possible by the internet it is no wonder that a lot more people are even searching for love on the internet. Is everyone just that busy that they can't mix and mingle in person?

Match.com

Looking for a match. At some point, I would assume that we all are looking for that counterpart to live our lives, share our dreams and grow old with. Now the internet has made this most convenient. Instead of getting dressed and leaving the house, you can sit in front of your laptop in your underwear and scratching your armpits while meeting the love of your life. I'm not sure this is good. In fact, I'd venture off to say this is a declining force in our society. The means of communicating are always evolving, but now personal interaction is almost taken out of the equation. This cannot be healthy.

Numbers Game

According to a study led by the University of Chicago's Department of Psychology, more than 1/3 of people married between 2005-2012 met their mate online. More than 1/3. With the presence of new online dating sites and the comfort level of people using online dating, the number may actually be surpassing that today. Not too long ago, it was frowned upon. These days, life has become so demanding and people have become so strangled for time that online dating has not only become more acceptable, but it has almost become a viable replacement for meeting people in person.

Where Did You Meet?

Call me old fashioned, but I think online dating takes away from the art of dating. It makes things too easy. Of course, people will say that easy is what they need because the rest of their life is so complicated. I am just afraid that with all of the communication being via online profiles initially that people will lose their ability to communicate in person. There may be some comfort or confidence in responding online, but will that person have that same confidence in person? Those are the intangible things that only physical interaction can bring about. I fear that in a world where so much communication is electronic and impersonal at least we would go out and meet people. Once you take that away, what remains?

Gloves Off

Over twenty years ago, the trial of OJ Simpson came to an end. Simpson was found not guilty of the murders of two people. One his ex-wife, Nicole Brown Simpson and the other was Ronald Goldman. The two were brutally murdered with several stab wounds to every area of the body imaginable. Yet through testimonies and lack of evidence Simpson was found not guilty.

If It Don't Fit

In the closing arguments, the famous line by attorney Johnnie Cochran was "If it doesn't fit you must acquit." And of course the gloves did not fit. But that's not the only thing that doesn't fit in this trial. The actions of the LAPD did not fit either, at least in the eyes of the watching world.

However, the truth is that the LAPD had been known for corruption and botched investigations. The only thing is that the natives knew this and now the whole world would find out. I guess the lingering idea though is what if Simpson actually did do it?

The World We Live In

Is it possible that OJ did brutally murder two people with so many stab wounds that it almost seemed impossible that one person would be capable of committing this crime unless the second person waited their turn before taking knife wounds? The fact remains though, that if there had not been so much corruption, racism and mishandling, perhaps the prosecution could have proven their case. Everything is merely speculation at this point because he was found not guilty, but the American people that watched and listened to the verdict found themselves guilty.

Hung Jury

As the verdict was read, a clear divide among most black and white viewers showed that we were still guilty of a racial divide in America. As much as we try to avoid or even act as though it does not exist, there is still a separation between the two and the verdict proved this to be true. A lot of whites thought Simpson to be guilty and felt as though he had somehow cheated the system. I find that laughable only because in hundreds of years we have never been able to thwart the judicial and legal system that was utterly created without us in mind in the first place. A lot of black people were happy about the verdict, but I think it gave us the wrong perception. Black people were not happy that we thought Simpson got away with murder. We were happy because for a moment it felt as though the law system had for once worked in our favor. Remember just three years prior a man was beaten by several police officers caught on video and they were all acquitted, right there in LA.

Black Voices

As a student at Adrian College, a small private college in Adrian, Michigan, I majored in journalism. Unfortunately there was no concentration on journalism in the communications curriculum. With that being the case, I had taken a vast allotment of communications courses including film history. Looking back on those communications classes sparked a synapsis in my brain that just will not retire to a small corner and lay dormant.

Talk The Talk

How important is the black voice? If history is our lesson, it would appear that the black voice is not only unimportant, but highly scrutinized. However, if you look beneath the surface you'll be faced with the realization that the black voice is indeed the polar opposite. The black voice is one that is so powerful, so truthful, that it compels some to give their most valiant efforts in trying to shut the vault on it so no one can ever hear it. When I say black voice, I'm not speaking of the vernacular. I'm talking about the substance of what those black voices are saying.

All My Dogs Barking

The black voice. No matter how extreme the measures of those who try to contain it, the shell is cracked away until it shines bright again. A great example of this is Arsenio Hall. A pioneer in black talk show hosts. Of course there was Oprah at the time, but you'll excuse me if I don't include her. I am thankful for her contribution to our culture and media, but let's be honest, how many black people in my generation vibe with Oprah. All that aside, Hall introduced the world to the dog pound. A section in the studio audience that stood and pumped their fists while barking like dogs. It was comical. However, as asinine as it seemed, it transcended racial boundaries. I think this was most apparent when Julia Roberts demonstrated the dog pound chant in a scene in Pretty Woman. That is when I understood that the black voice wasn't only strong and powerful, but it was something everyone wanted to encounter whether they admit to it or not.

Hall Of Fame

Hall brought the black voice to America's living room every night. This would be the first talk show to have, what was coined "gangsta rappers," interviewed on the show and perform as well. It was a winning formula because although America has historically dismissed us, the country is always so intrigued to hear what we have to say. That is the case...until our voice becomes too powerful. Hall's show ran from January 1989 until May of 1994. There were 1,406 shows with notable guests like Ali, Mike Tyson, NWA, Tupac Shakur and even Minister Farrakhan. Perhaps Hall was giving the world too much of our voice so it had to be silenced. I can still hear the dog pound though... woof... woof... woof... woof... pumping their fists in excitement. Our voices live on.

Nuking Our Brains

The microwave. I have always thought it was the worst invention ever. Sure you're able to nuke food in seconds. Of course almost every food imaginable has some sort of microwavable portion that makes it easy for the average Joe to become a chef in seconds. That's not why I dislike the microwave, by no means, because I have heated up many a leftover in my day using this device. It's the idea of the microwave that puts me on edge.

Done In Sixty Seconds

Ever since the microwave, we've been conditioned to think that things can always happen faster. People want the popcorn to be done before they hit the start button. People want money before they cash a check. Everybody wants everything now. Thanks to the microwave. It's humorous, but true. This is why our younger generation thinks it can have success and fortune without hard work and education.

Do The Math

Life is not microwaveable. I was watching an interview of Master P, or Percy Miller, and he was commenting on how No Limit got their first distribution deal. He attributed some success to the hustle that the streets of New Orleans had taught him. However, he stood behind his studies at the University of Houston where he studied business. Miller said that it was the things he learned about business in school that gave him the edge in negotiating the distribution deal as well as contributed to his first businesses. He stressed the importance of what he had learned in school.

Ditching Class

Unfortunately in some urban neighborhoods, it's not considered the cool thing to be smart. This is a stigma that needs to change within our community in order for us to progress as a whole as opposed to the select few that make it out and venture into the real world. I know that some will complain that the resources are not available and I would have to say that this is the furthest thing from the truth. In fact, there are many resources for education that go unused for so long that the funding disappears. So, in essence, it's not that they weren't available, it's just that the community has taken so little advantage of it that the funding stops and the programs become defunct.

Ahead Of The Class

It is evident how important an education is in this day and age. Especially since now the administration is pushing to make community college free. This is the first notion that reminds us that a high school education cannot be the highest education one has in order to proceed up the class ladder. Of course, some entrepreneurs would disagree, but even for the entrepreneur, there is some sort of education required to ensure their business stays afloat. Our community is in dire need of recognizing this. We are already starting from a handicapped position. As unfortunate as it is, it is the case. So, ditch the microwave lifestyle and choose the conventional oven directions and feed your brain. Aside from popular belief, it's not cool to be dumb.

The Witches' Brew

Over three hundred years ago, the Salem Witch Trials claimed the lives of over 20 men and women accused of witchcraft. They were executed as people in the town feared that these people possessed witchcraft powers. They were afraid. So they reacted the way humans react when they are afraid.

Who Are The Witches Now?

Fast forward to the future. People are still afraid of the unknown. Oddly enough, the African American has proven to still be amongst the unknown. After hundreds of years of captivity, hundreds of years of oppression and hundreds of years of mental captivity, somehow our mysterious souls are still feared. This must be the case. How else can you explain unarmed black citizens of this great country being gunned down in their vehicles while reaching for license and registration? How else can you explain a black man being beat nearly unconscious by white police officers on clear video footage and nobody spends one night in jail for this man's torture?

Fear Not

Perhaps it is because when our culture of people truly realizes what power we have had in the past and what power we are capable of having in the future, then the trivial means by which we have lived by thus far will explode into the reign of dynasties that we once ruled in Africa before being brought to America. I use the term brought cautiously, because we were not brought. We were enslaved, murdered and castrated in the transition. Nevertheless, here we are hundreds of years later as the witches of Salem.

The Trials

The Salem Witch Trials also inspired playwright Arthur Miller to pen "The Crucible," a play that received a Tony

Award in 1953. Indeed the play was intriguing because of the story it told of the witch trials, but even more so intriguing because at that time you could simply exchange black people for the witches in the story and the same rules would apply. The innate fear of the black American or fear of his potential undoubtedly spurs the actions of our society, especially law enforcement.

The Law Of The Land

For many years, probably since the inception of these United States Of America, there has been moves made motivated by fear. Perhaps that is even the original thinking behind laws. Laws were more than likely made to reduce fear among the cohabitants of a municipality, then of course through history have come into fruition as common policies that just make sense. However, the question is when do these laws serve as a double edge sword? The answer is easy. The laws protect the people, but sometimes are used to subdue the people at the same time. There were laws present at the time of the Salem Witch Trials, but somehow these laws allowed for the hanging and false imprisonment of several people. Sounds familiar doesn't it?

Getting To The Root

Violence and anger are most often the stigma of African Americans. The sad thing though, is that we are not doing much to avoid that stigma. In fact, we feed into the stereotype so often that it causes one to think that perhaps this is not a stigma. Perhaps it is the definition of our community. Sometimes I just wonder... what are we thinking?

Rosa Parks

Years after Rosa Parks stood her ground by sitting at the front of the bus, I think that our younger generation has forgotten the trials and tribulations that afforded them the right to ride the bus safely in the rear or in the front. I say that because here, where people boycotted to gain our Civil Rights, black people contribute to America's stereotyping of our community. A few months ago in Detroit, a 29-year old woman fatally wounded a 50 year-old woman after an altercation that started allegedly because the 50 year-old woman bumped her with her walker. Yes I said walker. The 29 year old suspect turned herself in after the incident. What are we thinking?

The Struggle Within

Now the details are few between at this point, but I am alarmed regardless. The fact is that an African American woman is dead from the fatal stab wounds of another African American woman. When white police officers kill people in our black communities we are outraged. We stand on our soapboxes and preach the gospel to anyone who will listen. Well who is preaching that gospel to us? What society do we live in when we are fighting for justice for the innocent people who parish at the hands of roguish law enforcement but have the audacity to murder one another in the same breath? I'm dumbfounded.

The Roots of Our Problems

I'd be inclined to say that years of oppression have led to generations of black people who garner intense hatred. But the hatred is not focused on who you would think most obvious. Our aggression and hatred has somehow focused on ourselves. When you are able to stab a 50 year old woman to death because of an altercation, then there is definitely some self-hatred going on there. There has got to be some inner aggression that allows one to react in such a savage manner to an elder. The most disheartening thing is that our younger generations don't respect elders or authority.

Respect Is Not Just an Aretha Franklin Song

Respect for ourselves, respect for our elders and respect for authority are key missing elements to the black community. How can we even confront the racial profiling and injustices of the world when we can't contain our own internal madness? I'm outdone to an extent that is immeasurable. How can we take to Facebook and Twitter about Trayvon Martin, Michael Brown and Sandra Bland but allow a woman to be killed while trying to ride the bus on Grand

River in her own community? So now I
don't want to be pulled over by the police
and I don't want my mother, grandmother,
auntie or sister riding the bus. I may be shot
to death for pulling out my registration and
my mother may be killed trying to get a
good seat on the bus. It is a hell of a battle
when you have to fight the opposing team
and fight your own teammates in the locker
room. At some point we all have to get on
the same page so we can run out of the
locker room and take the field together in
order to have a fighting chance against our
opposition. I'm just not sure if we will ever
make it out of the locker room.

Crossing The Lines

With presidential candidates playing hop
scotch from state to state declaring their
plans to make America great again, the
American citizens try to figure out just who
is going to be suitable to pick up where
President Obama has left off. There are

many major issues that concern the American citizens, but one of the hot topics is actually about American citizenship itself.

Boarder Line Politics

The boarders are a hot topic. Many citizens of America complain about lax immigration laws and minimal border patrol. In fact even when the Pope visited a few months ago, he addressed the Congress in hopes of changing the tone of the immigration argument. The Pope suggest that people who leave other places and come here to find opportunity and a better way of life should be granted the opportunity. Although the Pope's message is a breath of fresh air for people who agree, the congress and other opposition are fighting for stiffer laws to keep our borders closed.

The Numbers

Aside from Donald Trump throwing around numbers like 30 million in reference to illegal immigrants, reports show that the number of migrants in the US illegally are at 11.3 million and has been stable around that same number for the last few years. With this being said, people like Trump are exaggerating the numbers and giving US citizens imaginary ammo to use in the debate over immigration laws.

Got That Work

Another interesting fact about illegal immigrants is that reportedly they account for 5.1% of the US labor force. This is interesting because the argument normally from people wanting to cast out illegal immigrants is that they are getting benefits from a government that does not recognize them as citizens, when in fact they are working and contributing to the American work force. Most often doing jobs that most citizens would turn their noses up at or feel as though the work was beneath them.

What's Really Going On?

Immigration has been an issue for years, even more so a few years ago when it peaked in 2012 at over 12 million. But is the government really looking to tighten the borders? In all honesty there is a lot of drug trafficking that happens at the borders and somehow I don't believe this is something the government truly wants to disturb. Of course there is always some war against drugs, but realistically drug sales contributes to the American economy which is probably why so many states are hesitant to make marijuana legal. So maybe the borders are an issue for citizens, but not really for government. They'll just keep pretending it is so we won't see what's really going on.

Truth

In 1995, Minister Louis Farrakhan called on a million black men to come together in Washington, DC. for a message of atonement. Farrakhan was motivated to bring the black men together because we are the leader of our community and what better way to get the black community in order than to reform its leadership? Twenty years later, a reunion happened, but how have we done so far?

Two Decades In The Making

After the first Million Man March, there were many rejuvenated souls who took their learnings and aspiration of unity back to the neighborhoods in which they came. For a while it seemed to be effective. The black community had gotten a new awareness. A couple years later though, the deaths of rappers Tupac Shakur and Biggie Smalls along with the deaths of many nameless black young men across the nation proved that the black community had not yet taken heed of Farrakhan's message.

America's Role

As important as Farrakhan's message was to the black community, it was tainted with media outlets and even President Clinton. By this I mean white America attacked the integrity and purpose of Farrakhan. This may not sound major initially, but how do you think information is destroyed? The first way to destroy information is to make the receiver distrust the information's source. America wanted us to be upset because women were not invited. America wanted us to be upset that Farrakhan is a Muslim. America wanted us to discredit the source so that we would never receive the message. Sounds familiar doesn't it?

Willie Lynch

It's been a plan of destruction since the eve of the colonies that led to these United States of America. The black men and women were never a part of the grand scheme of things. Now that message was prepared to be delivered and of course the powers that be wanted to stop that flow of information. Our community is thirsty for this knowledge because as far back as the Willie Lynch Letter, we have been conditioned. Conditioned in a manner that depreciates our true value and has become so innate that we believe it unknowingly. We fall victim to control without even realizing it.

Broken Dreams and Broken Levees

Ten years later we remember the wrath of Hurricane Katrina. Katrina devastated the Gulf Coast and left many homeless. In fact some areas were completely displaced. Grounds that at one point were covered by neighborhoods looked as if civilization had never populated the area.

Katrina's 10 Year Anniversary

Images of ruined homes and disparity flooded the airwaves and internet. Families were displaced and lives were lost. To this date, there are families that have never returned to the place they once called home. Images of the Louisiana Superdome are present in several pictures as the streets filled with cars heading out of town. The foreshadowing of those images is nothing anyone would have guessed, but as the Superdome positioned itself in the background of several pictures it would soon become the focal point as the storm depleted everything in its path.

Nothing Super About The Superdome

Many held on to what they could and attempted to seek shelter inside the Superdome. It wasn't long after that when I realized, after seeing the people atop roofs of houses that were submerged in flood water so deep that only the very tops of the roofs were visible, that this was indeed a catastrophe. Inside the Superdome with no power or working plumbing, reportedly over 14,000 people tried to avoid the wrath of Katrina. Outside, neighborhoods were being washed away and families were being dismantled as loved ones went missing and others perished in the winds and waters of the storm. But, the question in my head still remains...was it handled properly?

One Bush in the Water

Aside from the images of neighborhoods and families being destroyed and water running through the streets like a leaky faucet, the image that resonates the loudest with me is the image of President Bush hovering over New Orleans and never landing to re-assure the American people that this disaster was being handled in the best fashion. You see him peeking out the window before being whisked away from the disaster that left people on rooftops with banners pleading for help. That's the reason Kanye West said on LIVE television that George Bush doesn't care about black people. I am not the biggest Kanye West fan, but I felt where he was coming from. The government did not seem to be in a particular rush to aid the worst hit portion of New Orleans, which just so happened to be consistent of economically challenged black people. In addition to that, it was not at all helpful that the media started referring to the displaced people and families as "refugees." In my head refugees usually meant people who don't actually belong here. Is that what they were trying to be remind us?

The Will To Move On

The people of New Orleans had the strength to move pass this historic moment and even though a lot of lives were lost, a lot of money was squandered and numerous families were displaced, they have marched forward. Some are in different states. Some were able to come back home and rebuild. In my heart though, the neighborhoods are not the only things that needed to be rebuilt. There is a bridge between the black community and the government – and now law enforcement – that is desperately in need of repair. Although the people have moved on, they have not forgotten the feeling of being left behind in a country that sometimes reminds us that we are not always particularly welcome. The moment we think the bridge is being repaired, we are often reminded and we definitely will never forget.

Hitler's Motive

The Black Hebrew Israelites. This is what a growing number of African Americans refer to themselves as in reference to the original

Hebrew people as being black in the biblical era. It is not a new idea, in fact, according to many stories in the bible, the growing group of Black Hebrew Israelites will attest that the truth has been given to us a very long time ago.

The Fuhrer

The interesting fact is that the Fuhrer, or more commonly known as Adolf Hitler, shared this same sentiment. The Nazi movement was ultimately fueled by the assumption that Jewish people had somehow taken on the role of the original Hebrew Israelites when in fact they were not. The atrocities that ensued during the Nazi movement sacrificed millions of Jewish lives as the Fuhrer led his army forward. The scary idea of it all though is that his theory is not much different than the Black Hebrew Israelites. The ideology that is presented here is that Jewish people have somehow pulled the vale over our eyes while pretending to be descendants of the original Hebrew people when it may not be the case at all. There are quite a few compelling arguments that make the "Jewish

Lie" theory believable including incidents in the bible itself. So, black people and Hitler have the same ideas? That's a scary thought all in itself.

Our New World Order

Hitler died during World War II. Reportedly he committed suicide inside his bunker after fearing being captured. Wait, no that's not what happened at all. He delivered a fatal gunshot to himself to end his life. Or did he? Some declassified FBI files have even been made available outlining the distinct possibility that Hitler's death had been faked, yet there was never any investigation by our FBI. Could this be because the United States somehow had a hand in Hitler and the Nazis rampage? Ironically there is a Nazi bunker off the beaten path rusting away right here in America in California. Did the government secretly aide Hitler's movement then allow him to fake his death and give us an imaginary victory against a Nazi organization that we had initially given the life to grow into what it had in the first place?

The X Is For Unknown

The US Government has a way of making things go away. I think we are all aware of this. However the frightening thing about this is that the government takes credit, sometimes anyway, for making things go away, but secretly they are the ones creating the very thing they are supposedly getting rid of. Is it because people are getting to close to the truth? Will Black Hebrew Israelites be stomped out by the government because it brings back the same ideology that Hitler proposed many years ago or will their voice be averted because it brings about the truth that nobody really wants us to know as black people because they know knowledge is power?

Keep The Faith

I heard some disturbing news from my hometown a while back. There was a pastor in Detroit, who shot and killed a man at the church. There were so many things that went through my head that I could barely think straight. What I would find out next made things even worse.

Church Folks

Now originally, reports from Fox 2, a local station in the city, stated that the pastor shot a man wielding a weapon who was trying to attack him. Instantly, I figured some deranged soul was probably trying to rob the pastor. I mean, it has happened on more than one occasion in my hometown, so it's the first thing that came to my mind. Then I learned that not only was this not just some crazed individual, it was a member of the church. A member who in fact had a close relationship with his pastor at one point. The news report goes on to say that the pastor says he had been stalked by the member. Perhaps this was a plea to justify the shooting. Then more information began to develop.

The Preachers Wife...And Your Wife Too

It turns out that there was an alleged affair between the pastor and the member's wife. It was this that prompted the member, whose name was Deante Smith, 26, to confront Pastor Keon Allison, 36. The alleged affair is also said to have produced a child between the two that the pastor paid to abort. While all of this is alleged, it prompts two very important questions in my mind.

Faith and Fury

The first question is how much is one person's faith tested when a man who seemingly was trying to do the right thing by his wife is pushed to the edge after being betrayed by his pastor, who some say was more like a mentor and father figure to the man? It's an unsettling feeling when you see someone who was trying to do things according to the bible without succumbing to the world after being betrayed by this pastor who served as his portal of spirituality fall at the hands of that very man whom he at one point looked up to in admiration. Smith's family was in disbelief of the situation, while authorities scrambled through investigations to see if the pastor would be charged. Your faith is tested to the very fabric of your soul knowing that a man who has been betrayed in such a manner, especially by his pastor and ends up losing his wife as if he was truly the one at fault here. The second question may surprise you.

Pastor Packing in the Pews

Is it normal for the pastor to have a gun on him at service? The incident happened at 1:45pm officials said, this is 15 minutes into the 1:30pm service that was scheduled. So, are you saying that the pastor was about to be teaching the word of the Almighty with a pistol strapped to his waste under his Holy robe? This is a concern that nobody has seemed to address. Personally, I'm not comfortable with my pastor toting a pistol in the pulpit. To me that is no different than having a teacher in a room full of students with a 9mm on his belt trying to write the lesson on the chalk board. Regardless, there is a man who lost his life at the hands of a man who he once admired. A man who reportedly had betrayed the trust of a young man and ultimately took his life. I imagine that the pastor may have indeed feared for his life. I also believe that he feared for his life because he knew he had betrayed a man and hurt him so deeply that he may have believed that his karma had shown up at church that day. Now he has an even greater Judge to answer.

Boys To Men

This generation of young boys have quite a steep hill to climb to manhood. With this in mind the hill becomes even steeper once you add in the statistics. According to the US Census Bureau, 1 in four children are born in fatherless homes. Due partly in the decline of marriage. That 1 in 4 statistic doesn't account for children who have no father in their lives at all, but are not in the same household. These statistics count basically for unwed parents, since there is no defining statistic that measures the absence of a father all together, however it does beg the question of whether a single mother is capable of raising a boy into a man if she is raising him alone.

It's a Man's World

Of course the woman is a nurturer by nature, but when it comes to molding a boy into a man, nurturing is not going to cut it alone. Now, in all fairness, in the black community single mothers often deal with the loss of their children's fathers to an early grave or incarceration. This leaves some single mothers to find their way through the dark forest of raising a young man all on their own. Regardless of race, some fathers just choose to not be in their child's life. This coupled with the growing number of single parent homes points to certain disaster. The circumstance is sometimes unfair, but the absence of a positive male figure in the life of a young boy contributes greatly to his ineffectiveness as a man once he grows older.

It Takes A Village

Now, it doesn't always have to be the father himself, but I believe there is definitely a need for this figure to exist in order for a young boy to grow into a competent young man if his primary attendant is his mother. There are many single mothers who will beg to differ, but contrary to what they might say, I'm not convinced. I believe it is absolutely necessary for there to be some sort of positive male figure in the boy's life in order for him to ever make the successful transition. I often reflect on my sister who was a single mother after the father of her children passed away while they were young. Knowing that they needed to have positive male figures in their lives to aid them in their transformation from boys to men, I stepped in to help. These actions are necessary for all men, especially in the black community, to step in as male figures in the lives of boys in their family and their community.

The Fact Is

Jill Scott may have said it best when she said "I can do all of these things...but I still need you," in her song entitled "The Fact Is." And the fact is that it does take a man to raise a boy into a man. The scary thing, though is that some men come from their own situation where they themselves never had a positive male figure in their lives so in essence never learned to be men themselves. That, unfortunately, in my eyes is the deciding factor. So, no, I don't think a single mother is capable of raising a boy into a man without the influence of that child's father or at least some male figure in his life to help mold him into man who can in turn teach his son to be a man in the future.

Get Ready For His Return

I remember seeing the episode of Good Times when JJ painted a picture of Black Jesus. It really was just a portrait of Ned

The Wino, but the Evans family started to have good fortune while the portrait was hanging on the wall. Of course, the super righteous character of Florida Evans forbid them to keep the painting up, even though apparently it had brought them some kind of luck. But then again, maybe she was right. Because religion and faith have nothing to do with luck.

Black Jesus

Thirty five years later Aaron McGruder brings Black Jesus to television. Of course when you think about Aaron McGruder the first thing you think of is Boondocks. With this in mind you already know the envelope is going to be pushed so far that it's scary. Admittedly, the show started over a year ago and it took me until now to bring myself to watch it. I was afraid that it would be blasphemous to watch it. I laugh now at the idea, but I honestly did think that. I originally had no idea that Aaron McGruder was behind the project.   Had I known this I probably wouldn't have been so hesitant.

Straight Outta Compton

Black Jesus is set in modern day Compton. The premise is the same as in the bible though. Jesus is on a mission to spread love in the community and encourage people to follow him. Not much variation from the biblical story, yet of course it is modern day Compton. The show is actually pretty funny. It approaches the edge like so many familiar with Boondocks could imagine, but not the least bit as blasphemous as I originally feared.

It Comes From The Earth

Now the episode I did watch was showing Jesus preparing a vacant lot to create a community garden. In the garden though the people who followed him, obviously reminiscent of the disciples from the bible, are preparing to grow marijuana. Yes it was Jesus leading a crew to grow marijuana. I laughed. It was funny. I'm sure some may not find it funny, but it is satire and that's what McGruder does best. In between time he says things that are very similar to things Jesus said in the bible, just put into terms of modern day society, so I'm not at all perturbed by Black Jesus

Good Times

Thirty five years ago Florida Evans raised
all kind of hell, no pun intended, about black
Jesus. She said that no Jesus she knows was
black and that the portrait was blasphemous.
Years later, we're questioning that. Perhaps
Jesus was black. The description in the
bible definitely refutes the white Jesus that
we have come to symbolize. However, that's
a whole other story. I guess I'll catch up
with the 1st and second seasons and get
prepared for his return because he'll be
coming back soon. I'm talking about Black
Jesus. The show of course.

Blue And Red Flags

I remember seeing Game on Wendy
Williams talking about his new album a few
months. He revealed that the album would
be a double disc. One side red and the other
side blue. Game, who is from Compton and
openly represents the Blood gang, said that

his double disc was not to glorify gang culture but to educate people of its origin.

Back in the Day

Red flags and blue flags. Bloods and Crips. Gang culture is alive and active in LA and has been for many years. Back in the sixties a man by the name of Stanley "Tookie" Williams along with Raymond Washington started the Crips gang. The gangs allegedly got into numerous altercations with other gangs in the area and had become an intimidating force to be reckoned with. Reportedly a confrontation involving the Crips and Sylvester Scott and Benson Owens led to the creation of Piru and West Piru gangs respectively. These sets bonded together with other non-Crip gangs and formed what would be known as the Blood Gang. And from there the gang culture that we know now was spawned.

Blaxploitation

Amidst the gang culture reports have suggested that the CIA infused the black community with cocaine that eventually would end up as crack and devastate an entire culture. The government officials reportedly used the rival gangs to push the same drugs that eventually would be used against them to land several people in jail and others dead. The gang culture and drug distribution had ran so rampant, that the government then tried to use a war against drugs movement to stamp out the problem. Of course this was to no avail because the government was initially the force behind the drug epidemic anyway. Well, I'll just say that all signs lead to this theory.

Slavery

Can it be true that even after the Emancipation Proclamation, America would find a way to enslave us once again? I looked at Game on the Wendy Williams show and I saw evolution. The gang banger had grown and evolved. He gives back to his neighborhood and teaches a new generation that there is life beyond the blue and red rags. All the while, the gang culture is still alive and active in LA and other places around the US. The government and powers that be are still searching for the new age shackle to keep the black community from reaching the Promised Land. We just have to be smart enough to keep our eyes on the prize.

Quincy L. Lewis

ABOUT THE AUTHOR

Quincy L. Lewis is a gifted writer whose experiences coupled with influence from great writers such as Richard Wright, Langston Hughes and James Baldwin bring a refreshing classical edge and urban voice together to create an amazing literary experience.

www.ingramcontent.com/pod-product-compliance
Lightning Source LLC
Chambersburg PA
CBHW070523030426
42337CB00016B/2083